THE STORY OF THE MUNSTERS

AT

ETREUX, FESTUBERT, RUE DU BOIS AND HULLOCH

BY

MRS. VICTOR RICKARD

AUTHOR OF "DREGS," "THE LIGHT ABOVE THE CROSSROADS,"
"THE FRANTIC BOAST," "THE FIRE OF GREEN BOUGHS"

WITH AN INTRODUCTION BY
LORD DUNRAVEN
Honorary Colonel, 5th Royal Munster Fusiliers

HODDER AND STOUGHTON
LONDON   NEW YORK   TORONTO
MCMXVIII

DEDICATED TO

VICTOR RICKARD

AND HIS COMRADES IN ALL RANKS OF THE
MUNSTER FUSILIERS, WHO FOUGHT AND FELL
IN THE GREAT WAR, 1914–15

"One who never turned his back but marched breast
  forward,
Never doubted clouds would break,
Never dreamed, though right were worsted, wrong
  would triumph,
Held we fall to rise, are baffled to fight better, sleep
  to wake."

The shamrock, which forms part of the cap badge of the Royal Munster Fusiliers, was first introduced, in February 1915, by Lieut.-Colonel Rickard, in the Second Battalion, with the object of giving a distinctively Irish emblem to all ranks of the Regiment. It is now worn by all the battalions of the Munsters.

PREFACE

I SHOULD like to express my thanks to the officers of the Royal Munster Fusiliers, and also to the friends and relatives who have helped me to collect and arrange this book. In the following accounts of the engagements of Etreux, Festubert, Rue du Bois and Hulloch, I do not wish in any sense to appear as an historian; that task awaits far abler and more qualified hands. What follows has been threaded together as a little tribute to the men who gave their lives for an Ideal, and who were brave soldiers in the Great War.

The first three chapters of this book appeared in *New Ireland* during the summer of 1915, and were shortly afterwards republished by that paper, together with the supplementary letters, as *The Story of the Munsters*. A second impression was sold out by the end of the year, since when no copies of the book have been obtainable. The new features of the present edition are the historical Introduction specially written by Lord Dunraven, to whom my best thanks are due, and the four pictures and the account of the Munsters at Hulloch which have already appeared in *The Sphere*. Its Editor, Mr. Clement Shorter, has a special claim to the lasting gratitude of the Munster Fusiliers for the deep interest he has always shown in all records of the Regiment; and it is by his permission that the illustrations, which add incalculably to the slender story itself, are here reproduced. My thanks are also offered to Mr. Geddes, who has designed the colour plate on the cover, and brought into the book a sense of the traditions which surround the regimental flags.

L. RICKARD.

INTRODUCTION

THE origin of the Royal Munster Fusiliers, like that of those other great Irish Regiments, the Dublins and the Leinsters, is inextricably bound up with those great movements of Imperial expansion which took place in the eighteenth century. Of the Leinsters one battalion was originally raised in Canada and another in India. Both regular battalions of the Dublins were raised in India. Like them, the 1st and 2nd Battalions of the Royal Munsters (before the Caldwell reconstruction the 101st and 104th Foot) were originally regiments in the army of the East India Company, raised out of British-born volunteers in India and only taken over as part of the British Army when the control of India passed from the Company to the Crown. It is for this reason that on the grenade which, in common with other Fusilier battalions, is worn by the Munsters the royal tiger of India is superimposed.

Until the present war, with the exception of the notable service performed by the 1st Battalion in South Africa, all the battle honours of the Regiment come from India or the surrounding countries. The regimental colours record service for the 1st Battalion at the following actions: Plassey, Condore, Masulipatam, Badara, Buxar, Rohilcund, Carnatic, Sholinghur, Guzerat, Deig, Bhurtpore, Afghanistan, Ghuznee, Ferozeshah, Sobraon, Pegu, Delhi, Lucknow and Burmah; while for the 2nd Battalion, raised as we shall see eighty years after the first, there are the Punjaub, Chillianwallah, Goojerat, Pegu and Delhi. To trace these records in detail would be to write the history of the steps by which we acquired our Indian Empire. They explain sufficiently (with the regimental origin in the Company's forces) why there were no Munsters in the Napoleonic wars.

The 1st Battalion dates its corporate existence from the 22nd December, 1756, when Clive, who had just returned to India and was about to begin the most glorious epoch of his career, raised it under the title of the Bengal European Regiment. The Regiment fought in his army at Plassey and Condore and in every action of that war up to the great victory of Buxar in October 1764. In 1779 it was sent to the Presidency of Madras and under Eyre Coote fought at Windeywash; in 1794 it took part under Abercrombey in the Rohilla wars; it was present (being known then, after the fashion of the India Army, by the name of its Colonel—

Clark's Corps) at the occupation of Macao in 1808. In 1839 it served in Afghanistan, when out of volunteers for it the 104th Regiment (now the 2nd Battalion Royal Munster Fusiliers) was formed. It served with distinction in the Sikh War, and as a reward for its services was raised to the dignity of a fusilier corps. The colours carried by the Regiment at this period hang in Winchester Cathedral. It went through all the fiercest engagements of the Mutiny and was present at the siege and capture of Lucknow. In 1861 it went under the Crown and became the 101st Regiment (Royal Bengal Fusiliers). From 1868 to 1874 it served in England, then abroad again, and in 1883 became the 1st Battalion Royal Munster Fusiliers. In 1899 it had the distinction of being sent to South Africa from Fermoy before mobilisation, being the first home regiment to go out to

INTRODUCTION

the war. It served with great distinction in Lord Methuen's force at Belmont, and afterwards on the march to Pretoria, and in the latter period of the war supplied a mounted infantry battalion.

The history of the 2nd Battalion is shorter, but no less glorious. Formed during the first Afghan War in 1839 out of surplus volunteers for its sister Battalion, it took part in the great victory of Chillianwallah, went through the Burmese War 1851-53, and in the Mutiny was part of the force which stormed Delhi. In 1861 it was brought into the line as the 104th Regiment, but served for ten years more in India before it came home. In 1887 it joined the Second Burmah Expedition, and like the 1st Battalion served with great distinction in the South African War in Natal, and later under Lord Kitchener in the Transvaal and Cape Colony.

INTRODUCTION

The 2nd Battalion was sent to France at the beginning of the present war. It suffered very severely and has been reinforced by the 3rd, 4th and 5th Battalions. The 1st, 6th and 7th Battalions have served at the Dardanelles, and after the evacuation of Gallipoli the 1st Battalion went to France. They have also suffered heavy losses. Both on the Western front and in the East the Regiment has splendidly maintained its ancient renown. To go further into modern history would be to trespass upon Mrs. Victor Rickard's admirable pages. I write these few lines about the origin of the Regiment because they may be interesting to her readers. We must not forget that though the bones come from Bengal, the blood and sinews are Irish. It is as an Irish regiment that the Munsters are celebrated in these pages. It is Irishmen who have won its new battle honours.

It is Irish men and women who have suffered, Irishmen who have triumphed in the field. The record of the Regiment is splendid, and I am proud to sign myself

DUNRAVEN,
Hon. Col. 5th Battalion,
Royal Munster Fusiliers.

CONTENTS

	PAGE
THE STAND OF THE MUNSTERS AT ETREUX	1
THE MUNSTERS AT FESTUBERT	17
THE MUNSTERS AT RUE DU BOIS	32
THE MUNSTERS AT HULLOCH	45
THE STAND AT ETREUX	55
APPENDIX	67

LIST OF ILLUSTRATIONS

THE MUNSTERS AT ETREUX
    (*Drawn by Christopher Clark*) To face page 1
MAJOR P. A. CHARRIER (*Photograph*)   ,,   6
THE MUNSTERS AT FESTUBERT
    (*Drawn by Philip Dadd*)   ,,   17
LT.-COL. A. M. BENT, C.M.G.
                   (*Photograph*)   ,,   24
LT.-COL. G. J. RYAN, D.S.O. (*Photograph*)   ,,   28
THE LAST ABSOLUTION AT RUE DU
  BOIS . (*Drawn by F. Matania*)   ,,   34
LT.-COL. V. G. H. RICKARD (*Photograph*)   ,,   38
CAPT. J. CAMPBELL-DICK (*Photograph*)   ,,   40
THE MUNSTERS AT HULLOCH
    (*Drawn by F. Matania*)   ,,   45
MAJOR J. W. CONSIDINE (*Photograph*)   ,,   49
MAPS TO ILLUSTRATE THE STAND OF
  THE MUNSTERS AT ETREUX (*Sketch A*) page 57
                             (*Sketch B*) ,, 63
OFFICERS OF THE 2ND RL. MUNSTER
  FUSILIERS, MAY 1915 (*Photograph*) To face page 66

Drawn by Christopher Clark.

THE MUNSTERS AT ETREUX, AUGUST 27TH, 1914

[*To face p.* 1.

THE STAND OF THE MUNSTERS AT ETREUX

August 27th, 1914

(WHICH TOOK PLACE DURING THE RETREAT FROM MONS)

"Then lift the flag of the last crusade,
And fill the ranks of the last brigade,
March on to the fields where the world's remade
And the ancient dreams come true."
　　"A Song of the Irish Armies." By T. M. Kettle.

On the 13th of August, 1914, the 2nd Battalion Royal Munster Fusiliers left Aldershot on their way to an unknown destination "somewhere in France."

The Expeditionary Force was reaching forward, as one of the officers wrote, towards "a jolly in Belgium," and he also added, "some of us will

2 STORY OF THE MUNSTERS

not come back." The same joy that was with Garibaldi and his thousand when they went forth to the redemption of a small and gallant race, went, we all know, with the men of the First Division. Each one knew that an hour lay ahead when great issues were to be joined, and the Munsters were proud to feel that the chance was with them to add to the records of their Regimental history.

The Battalion embarked at Southampton, and the transport steamed out shortly after noon, arriving at Le Havre at 3 a.m. on the 14th of August. From there they marched to a rest camp on the ridge west of Harfleur, where they remained until the 16th of August, and once more they marched to Havre, where they entrained for the concentration area at Le Nouvion. On Sunday, the 17th, Le Nouvion was crowded with French troops, and the townsfolk, wild

STORY OF THE MUNSTERS

with enthusiasm, welcomed the Munsters, and from thence the Regiment marched to Bouey, three miles distant from Etreux. The dawn of the 22nd of August saw the Battalion on the road again, marching towards Mons.

All of this is now like the fragment of a dream, and the troops who marched and sang are many of them on the further side of the boundary; but still the memory remains, though the rows and ranks of men are gone, and, like the clerk in the old story, "Come to Oxford and their friends no more."

> "It's a long way to Tipperary,
> A long wa-ay to go."

. . . . . .

All round and about Chapeau Rouge, a village near the river Sambre, and not far from Le Cateau, the country is a bower of green hedgerows in the month of August. In ordinary times, when trenches, deeper than any grave, and wire entanglements, and all the devastation of war is not, a country cut up into small fields has an intimate and friendly look. It suggests little things, and is small and near and has none of the sudden desolation of open space, stretching empty to the sky line. But what is beautiful in times of peace may in one moment become terrible in time of war, and the little hedgerows cost Ireland dear on the morning of the 27th of August, 1914.

The morning broke sullen and heavy, and the distant electric premonition of coming storm and coming battle vibrated in the air. The Munsters were placed as the Right Battalion, next to them came the Coldstream, further on the Scots Guards, with the Black Watch in reserve. The frontage of the Munsters extended from Chapeau Rouge, where the roads crossed, to another cross roads north of Fesmy.

Major Charrier (commanding the Munsters) had explicit orders to hold the cross roads above Chapeau Rouge, unless or until he received orders to retire. Dawn found the men of B Company, commanded by Captain Simms, busily digging trenches and strengthening their position, while the air was comparatively cool.

The German attack was expected in the course of the morning, and B Company was the first company of the Battalion to receive its baptism of fire.

For men whose record shows them proud, fiery, and dashing soldiers, the task alloted to B Company was no easy one. It was necessary that their position should be kept secret, and when at last the crackle and rattle of German musketry broke the tension of this waiting, the Company holding the outpost did not reply. The German patrol, whose business it was to locate their position, kept up an intermittent fire, and the small handful of Irish did the hardest thing of all for them—they waited. The lulls and bursts followed one upon the other; tremendous echoes repeated the volleys of sound, and the swinging shrill of flying bullets continued overhead, punctuated now and again by spells of intense quiet.

Suddenly the midsummer storm broke with a violence that is indescribable. Torrents of drenching rain soaked the men to the skin and collected in the trenches, and in the vortex of the storm the Germans advanced to the attack. In one moment it was " War, war, bloody war," and the first onslaught fell upon B Company, and D Company (commanded by Captain Jervis) with Lieutenant Crozier and Lieutenant R. W. Thomas.

The Munsters repelled the attack with fierce determination, and the little

MAJOR P. A. CHARRIER
2nd Royal Munster Fusiliers, killed at the head of his Battalion
at Etreux, near Mons, August 27th, 1914

Record of Service :—West Africa, 1900—Operations in Ashanti, slightly wounded ; Despatches, London Gazette, 8th March, 1901. South African War, 1902—Employed with Imperial Yeomanry operations in Cape Colony, May, 1902. Queen's Medal, with two clasps. East Africa, 1903-4—Operations in Somaliland on Staff (as Special Service Officer). Employed on Transport (from November, 1903). Medal, with clasp.

[*To face p.* 6.

fields around Chapeau Rouge became a place of violent and terrible memory, but the men held doggedly to their position until the order came to withdraw a mile to the rear. B Company was at this point detailed to act as right flank guard on the east, where the attack was hottest, and in endeavouring to carry out this order, they were cut off from the flank by the thick green hedgerows, and so to them came the adventure of maintaining a little battle of their own.

The rain continued and the mud grew deep, and very slowly and without heavy loss B Company fell back through Fesmy, fighting through the small wide street until it rejoined the Battalion on the further side. They had shaken the Germans off for the moment in spite of their immensely superior numbers, and had done most gallantly. After a short delay Major

Charrier sent them to take the head of the column and march to Oisy as advance guard.

The day continued showery for some hours, with occasional drenching bursts, but the men cared nothing for the discomfort of soaked clothes. It has been decreed by the Power that rules the destiny of men and nations that the call of a bugle makes the heart of Ireland glad. There was real adventure in their lives that morning ; the actual vital essence of it was touched by the rank and file of the marching men, for abstract safety as a condition to be desired has never entered very much into the Celtic vision of what life can give in those moments when it is at its best.

From Fesmy the Munsters pushed on to Etreux, there to join the main body of troops holding that town.

. . . . . .

Up the wide road where the bridge at Oisy spans the curve of the river Sambre, and some miles from where the Munsters were retiring towards Etreux, about sixty men of the Battalion, under Captain Emerson, took up their position, hoping to hold the road. They were here reinforced by the Coldstream Guards, who were endeavouring to get into touch with the Munsters, now separated from them by five miles of road, upon which the enemy were advancing rapidly.

To the meadow near the bridge where the Munsters were collected an orderly carrying a dispatch came up at about three o'clock in the afternoon. The time of the dispatch was not marked upon the message, which was to order the Munsters to retire "at once." The orderly who carried the message had, he said, been chased by the enemy, and after lying hidden for a time under the nearest cover, believed that it was not possible for him to bring the message through to Major Charrier. Upon this incident the tragedy of the whole day turned. Time had been lost, time too precious ever to regain ; the exclusive supremacy is nearly always a question of minutes.

Colonel Ponsonby decided that it was best to retire the Coldstreams and the handful of Munsters who were with them, and these were joined some miles back by Captain Woods and seventy men, who had fallen back to the Guise road.

. . . . . .

The river Sambre is full of curves, and winds past Fesmy and Etreux. Just along the right bank there runs a railway line, turning through a deep cutting into the station of Etreux. From there, the old you or I who lived before the war could have travelled comfortably across three frontiers in a few short hours. In this pastoral country, surrounded at evening by the softness of rising damp, stands Etreux, but none of the wandering fortunes of life will ever carry anyone back to look at the same picture any more.

When the Munsters marched onwards the early evening was bright again, and the heavy clouds had rolled to westward. The little environs stretched out along the road; a few houses, a cabaret, an orchard bright with cider apples, some already collected in piles under the trees; further again another proud house, bigger than the rest, and then streets, a palisade of trees and a spire. All this seen at a glance, where the road passed the railway cutting; for in the month of August war had not yet made France hag-ridden and desolate. Near to the railway cutting, and on the rise of ground a cross marked a turn to a side road, and a number of tiny lath crosses stuck into the grass signified that the good folk of Etreux carried their dead that way. Beneath the high cross was written "Ave Crux Spes Unica," and its shadow fell over the road, dividing the Munsters from the village like the boundary of a frontier.

Within a few yards of the outlying buildings, a sudden burst of rifle and artillery fire swept through the ranks of the Regiment, informing them finally and terribly that they were cut off. The men rallied magnificently, and B Company extended at once. Led by Captain Simms, they went forward to attack the enemy's main position, which was in the loopholed house that dominated the road. The railway cutting was held in force by the Germans, and D Company, commanded by Captain Jervis, and covered by the steady rifle fire of the men in position by one of the fields on the side of the road, rushed the railway cutting. Every man save two were shot down in the attempt; Lieutenant Crozier, showing the greatest gallantry, crossed a narrow lane, and exposing himself recklessly to the enemy's fire, shouted, "There they are; come on, men," and fell, killed instantaneously. The rattle of musketry, the booming of guns speaking terribly, was everywhere; the air itself vibrated and the ghastly transformation which men call war, continued. Everywhere the dead lay in huddled heaps, and the wounded with grey faces tried to rise, or crawled in maimed agony a little further on to die.

Bit by bit the shattered remnant of the Battalion fell back into the orchard, where Captain Chute brought the machine guns along the road under a hail of lead, and placed them in position. He was wounded in the side, and immediately afterwards was killed by another bullet.

Led by Major Charrier, the Munsters charged and charged again, against the enveloping force which now circled them around with a ring of fire, dropping shells and bullets. Major Charrier, who was twice wounded, steadily continued the direction of the action. He was standing by one of the guns which had been put out of action when Lieutenant Gower came and reported to him, just about sunset. Once more he rallied the men to the charge, and mortally wounded, he fell as they crossed the road.

Incident by incident the later stages of the heroic stand developed as the hours passed on, and ammunition could only be renewed by taking what was left on the dead and dying, and moment after moment gave fresh hostages to death.

Slowly and dreadfully the twilight came as the German onslaught gathered force, and the many sounds of battle rose and rose around the men who, with the Battalion thinned to less than half their fighting forces, still resisted the massed battalions of German soldiers; but the Munsters gave themselves with courage and lavishness, strong and unconsciously splendid. Once more they charged, and the great seas of uncounted enemy's troops crushed and broke them and forced those who were left to surrender.

So the bitterest hour of all was the last.

. . . . . .

It is told that the German officers said that men had never fought more bravely; it is also said that they sent back to their headquarters for a chaplain to bury the Irish dead.

Major Charrier and eight officers of

the Munsters were buried near the trench where the men were laid to rest, under the shadow of the trees where they had fought their great fight. But though we call them dead, we know that the spirit that is strong and cheerful, and that has added to the page of a nation's history, outlives all so-called untimely endings. The finished work, the completed undertaking, is not for many in the story of this great war, and it is not a little thing but a fine deed, to have left a record that betters the honourable traditions of the Royal Munster Fusiliers.

" Dying ye shall die greatly with a glory that shall surpass the glories of the past."

THE MUNSTERS AT FESTUBERT
December 22nd, 1914

Drawn by Philip Dadd.] [*To face p. 17*

THE MUNSTERS AT FESTUBERT

December 22nd, 1914.

"Your ashes o'er the flats of France are scattered,
  But hold a fire more hot than flesh of ours.
The stainless flag that flutters frayed and tattered,
  Shall wave and wave like spring's immortal flowers.
You die, but in your death life grows intenser,
  You shall not know the shame of growing old.
In endless joy you wave the holy censer,
  And blow a trumpet though your lips are cold."

"To Our Dead." By EDMUND GOSSE.

ON the evening of the 20th December, 1914, the 2nd Battalion Royal Munster Fusiliers, commanded by Colonel A. M. Bent, were billeted in the outskirts of Bailleul. They were scattered about in the farm houses and barns, in the narrow, yellow-plastered châteaus, that let in all the draughts from all the corners of the country, and in the little villa houses on the threshold of Bailleul itself.

Up to that time Bailleul had escaped from the destruction of falling shells, and only the far-away boom of guns made war very strongly evident; that and the masses of British troops and the passing of motor transport, divorced it from its old dreaming quiet of a few months back. The weather was intensely cold; an icy west wind came over the frozen flats, and drove the tearing rain-storms out of the mist-covered fens.

The Regiment had been some weeks in billets, re-equipping and training, going steadily through the process by which freshly drafted youngsters are made into fine soldiers. Colonel Bent was unusually gifted with the quality that inspires men to realise the value of central control; his personality and indomitable will made for an influence that the hundreds of men under his command responded to instinctively. Many of those who fought with him at Ypres and elsewhere have testified to this.

Previous to December 20th the Battalion had been " standing by " ready to move at the shortest notice, but on the morning of December 20th a message was received from Brigade Headquarters to the effect that the Battalion need no longer be held in readiness; so normal, semi-peace conditions reigned. They were, however, not destined to enjoy these conditions for long, nor to turn their thoughts towards the completion of Christmas festivities, for at 5 p.m. an urgent message was received by Colonel Bent that the 3rd Brigade, to which the Battalion belonged, was to be ready to march "as soon as possible."

It was quite dark when the order came, and though the men were scattered in their billets, at 6.15 p.m. the Munsters were in their place in the Brigade, and marching out into the stormy darkness. Behind them the dream of Christmas vanished like so many dreams. Reality took its place, a reality of a road ankle deep in mud, a tearing blizzard of rain and hail, and a black drenching tempest to face with bent heads.

For six hours the Battalion marched forward until at Merville a halt was called ; and in an empty factory there was rest and shelter for the drenched and weary men.

There was no sign anywhere of any promise of day in the sky ; it might have been the commencement of eternal night and of eternal darkness when the Munsters stood to arms. The men were heavy with their four hours' sleep, heavy, too, with their load of ammunition and equipment. They left the factory behind them and took the sodden road, and at last the ashen grey dawn broke, and the landscape slowly cleared from the shadow of night, but the rain never ceased nor lessened ; and the sound of the heavy guns told that the " business as usual " of the war had begun again.

At 8 a.m., outside Bethune, the Battalion halted again awaiting orders, the men sitting or lying in the mud along the roadside, keeping as cheerful as circumstances would permit. With his unwavering cheerfulness and energy, Colonel Bent worked against the conditions of the weather and the hardships his men were undergoing, affecting everyone with his own courage and dispelling the despondency of weariness,

22 STORY OF THE MUNSTERS

which is one of the hardest things a man can face. A battle itself calls up the human characteristics of dash and fight, but weariness and rain and mud are cruel adversaries, fought at a disadvantage. It is in those hours that most of all the magnetism of personality is of superb value. Afterwards, when the issue is no longer doubtful and the battle is over, and the definite, conspicuous end gained, it is easy for anyone to raise a cheer; but sitting in the liquid mud, weary and very cold, it takes a strong heart and the truest kind of pluck to rise above it all.

By 3 p.m. orders were received that the Battalion was to occupy the trenches at Festubert vacated by the Indian troops; the leading Brigade deployed for attack, and shortly after the Third Brigade were placed on the left of the First Guards Brigade. This Brigade consisted of the 2nd Welsh Regiment, the 1st Gloucesters, supported by the Munsters, the 1st South Wales Borderers, and the 4th Royal Welsh Fusiliers (Territorial). After the issue of these orders the Brigade resumed its march, through Gorre to Festubert, where the Battalion remained in reserve, but on the night of the 21st received orders that there was to be a general attack upon the German line.

All the night of the 21st the Munsters waited, and all the night of the 21st it rained and snowed and stormed.

. . . . . .

The pitch darkness of a night of waiting is a memorable experience, even when there are many such to record. There is the curious feeling of loneliness common to all humans out in the night. The bright smoke of fires over the land behind the parapets of the German trenches made will-o'-the-wisp columns of misty light; sometimes a star shell shot up, lighting the place like day, and sometimes the crack of a rifle tore the dark and spattered in the mud of the trench. Life and death come much closer in the night than they do in the day time, and the whole almost intolerable mystery of war is intensified a thousandfold. Very slowly the sullen dawn broke, as if unwilling to reveal the sights that night clothed over, and the sodden fields and the barns and farmsteads stood out blackly against the grey. The green and yellowish water lying over the flats was frozen, and the dead were very visible, lying in pathetic heaps amid the refuse of a thousand unexpected things. The weary desolation of dawn over French Flanders passes all description.

The noise grew with the morning light, and the boom and bang of heavy crashes grew fiercer, until the hour arrived when the Battalion,

LIEUTENANT-COLONEL A. M. BENT, C.M.G.
2nd Royal Munster Fusiliers, dangerously wounded at Festubert,
22nd December, 1914

Record of Service :—South African War, 1902—Operations in the Transvaal, January to April, 1902. Queen's Medal, with three clasps. North-West Frontier of India, 1908—Operations in Mohmand Country. Medal with clasp.

[*To face p.* 24.

led by Colonel Bent, started to the attack.

The men swarmed over the parapets and raced across the fields, carrying their heavy equipment and following their officers over the shell-scarred, churned-up earth. Strands of barbed wire beset their way, and the ground was broken by great shell-holes. Before them, from the German trenches, the machine guns hammered out their deadly message of welcome ; and the men went gamely on, most splendidly led by their officers.

Major Thomson, Second in Command, fell across the first German trench, but would not permit himself to be removed; continuing to issue orders from where he lay, he was wounded again, the second wound proving fatal. He met his death unvanquished and unappalled, and his name remains bound in with the great story of the Regiment. Colonel Bent fell in the earlier part of the charge, desperately wounded; Major Day was killed a little later, showing the greatest gallantry; and Captain Hugh O'Brien, a young Irish officer beloved by his men, and who had been proved in the South African War to possess unusual dash and coolness, fell as he shouted to his company, "Get a bit of your own back, boys." Not twenty yards from where Captain O'Brien fell Captain Durand met his death. He had joined the 3rd Battalion Royal Munster Fusiliers in 1906, having served through the Matabeleland and Mashonaland campaigns in the Rhodesian Horse; he died most nobly, leading at the extreme point of the advance made by C Company, under fierce enfilading fire. The sorrow and the heroism of such death is touched by the great enduring light of glory.

Men fell on the right and left, and again and again they rallied and stumbled over the broken ground, holding steadily on under the wail of tearing shrapnel, and at last the Munsters reached their goal, the given point ; and in the fierce counter attack they did not lose an inch of what they had taken.

So the day passed, and the wounded lay out under the cruel lash of the sleet and the bitter wind. Not one man returned to Headquarters, except some wounded who straggled in, dazed and bleeding. The chorus of the field guns, and the detonation of the great guns, and the crack, crack of rifle fire went on persistently. Lyddite and high explosives rained through the murky evening, and still no orders were issued that reached the Munster Fusiliers. They had gone out, as is their way, to do their bit, and had disappeared into the vast nothingness behind the night.

Darkness fell, and great flashes lit the dark ; those pale, awful gleams of super-civilisation swept over the ghastly land,

The enemy's search-lights were feeling after the mutilated and wounded, showing up the stretcher bearers and Red Cross dressers, and as each slow beam swung in its deadly course, a hail of lead followed it, bearing death on its coming.

In a big yawning gap of bog and dyke and mud the Munsters held on, unassisted, supports having failed. The Companies were lying out under fire, pinned to the ground, and with nearly all their officers killed or wounded, they still held on.

. . . . . .

Major Julian Ryan, D.S.O., who had gone back to Brigade Headquarters on the morning of the 22nd, to arrange about ammunition, and transport, as he put it himself in a letter, "sized up trouble" when "the Regiment disappeared into nothingness." It was he who left a record of the work done

LIEUTENANT-COLONEL G. J. RYAN, D.S.O.
2nd Royal Munster Fusiliers, killed near Festubert,
January 23rd, 1915

Record of Service:—South African War, 1899-1901—Employed with the Mounted Infantry, advance on Kimberley, including actions at Belmont and Modder River; operations in the Transvaal from June to 29th November, 1900; operations in Cape Colony, operations in the Transvaal, 30th November, 1900, to March, 1901; operations in Orange River Colony, March to June, 1901. Despatches, London Gazette, 10th September, 1901—Vaal, June to 29th November, 1900; operations in Cape Colony. Queen's Medal and five clasps, D.S.O. Soudan, 1905—Operations against the Nyam-Nyam tribes in Bahr-el-Gazel Province; Despatches, London Gazette, 18th May, 1906. Egyptian Medal Clasp. Soudan, 1906—Operations at Talodi in Southern Kordofan—Clasp to Egyptian Medal. Soudan, 1906—Operations in Blue Nile Province. Promoted Temporary Lieutenant-Colonel, London Gazette, 22nd January, 1915.

[*To face p.* 28.

by the six men of the search party to whose efforts, as to his own, the safe return of a single man of the Munster Fusiliers is chiefly due.

Having reported at Brigade Headquarters, and having received the reply that no help could be given, Major Ryan split his men into patrols of two and sent them out. At 8 p.m., when it was very dark and the enemy's fire unceasing, the men, whose names, unfortunately, are not recorded, came back reporting: "Very few officers left; many casualties; Colonel wounded; two senior Majors killed. Send orders." Major Ryan, fully aware that daybreak would see the end of the gallant Battalion if nothing were done, redoubled his efforts.

"It was 10 o'clock before the Brigadier's orders got to me to get orders out to the Battalion to retire, and even by then I had not a single unwounded man left of all the four companies that had gone out at 7 a.m. to show me where they had got to. Once more I called on my trusty six who had located them at dusk, and sent them out in three parties, again with definite orders to come back to me at a certain point where I was alone but for a few stray men and no officers. By midnight, to my relief, I got the remnant of the four companies in, worn out and starved, as their officers had fallen and many men, in the advance. All they could do was to follow my guides in. I called for volunteers and took a party out with stretchers and got some wounded in, but drew blank for the Colonel and Major Thomson. The Adjutant had come in unwounded, but dead beat, and could not say where the Colonel was.

"At 2 a.m., or nearly 3, I went round and collected the exhausted non-commissioned officers who had come in, called for volunteers again, and put the machine-gun officer in charge. The party returned carrying the Colonel wounded. All the rescue work was done under fire. . . . The Regiment did all, and more than all, that men could do ; they played up splendidly. I have never known men do so much. I am very proud of them."

A few weeks later Major Ryan, an officer of the most brilliant promise and striking personality, was killed by a sniper, to the great sorrow of the Battalion.

THE MUNSTERS AT RUE DU BOIS

May 9th, 1915.

"She, beyond shelter or station,
 She beyond limit or bar,
 Urges to slumberless speed
 Armies that famish and bleed,
 Giving their lives for her seed,
 That their dust may re-build her a Nation,
 That their souls may re-light her a star."
                    A. C. SWINBURNE.

ABOUT a mile from the market-place of Neuve Chapelle, and above Festubert and Givenchy, is the Rue du Bois, a street lying east and west, some 500 yards behind the British trenches. Last year the bells of Neuve Chapelle sent the sound swinging over the little distance, but the pounding of the shells

STORY OF THE MUNSTERS 33

of friend and enemy alike, silenced the bells, when war let loose the great stream of human blood and human tears. The Rue was once a thoroughfare for early carts and other traffic going towards the Distillery on the Violaines Road, and had been built according to the Roman system—one straight line of houses all built together. Along this street the carts used to pass, coming up from Richebourg St. Vaast and Richebourg l'Avoué, and going on by the road that leads to distant Lille. The Rue du Bois is now a sad place, for the chimney-stacks have fallen, and the roofs and walls gape desolately. Changed times for France since the early carts went by, and a changed world for many of us.

On the evening of Saturday, May 8th, 1915, the 2nd Royal Munster Fusiliers, commanded by Colonel Victor Rickard, were on their way to take their place in the trenches in front of Rue du Bois; with them was Father Francis Gleeson, whose name is known throughout the whole of Munster. It was a clear spring evening, dark under a green sky, the orchards through the country heavy with blossom, their scent recalling manifold recollections. The poplar trees, many of them shell-scarred and broken, were very still in the windless twilight, dark spires against the clear clean sky. At the entrance to the Rue du Bois there stands a broken shrine, and within the shrine is a crucifix.

When the Munsters came up the road, Colonel Rickard halted the Battalion. The men were ranged in three sides of a square, their green flags, embroidered with the Irish harp and the word " Munster," a gift from Lady Gordon, placed before each Company. Father Gleeson mounted, Colonel Rick-

Drawn by F. Matania.]

THE LAST ABSOLUTION OF THE MUNSTERS AT RUE DU BOIS, MAY 8TH, 1915

[To face p. 34

ard and Captain Filgate, the Adjutant on their chargers, were in the centre, and in that wonderful twilight Father Gleeson gave a General Absolution. To some present, very certainly, the "vitam æternam" was intensely and beautifully manifest, the day-spring of Eternity very near. "Miseratur vestri Omnipotens Deus, et dimissis peccatis vestris, perducat vos ad vitam æternam." The whole Regiment with their heads bared, sang the *Te Deum*, the great thanksgiving, the "Sursum Corda" of all the earth.

There are many journeys and many stopping-places in the strange pilgrimage we call life, but there is no other such journey in the world as the journey up a road on the eve of battle, and no stopping-place more holy than a wayside shrine.

The men who prayed there were, very few of them, the men of the original Battalion. Gaps had been filled again and again, and most of the Munsters who fought next day were newly come from Ireland and new to the life. Lads from Kerry and Cork, who, a year before, had never dreamed of marching in the ranks of the British Army.

The Regiment moved on, and darkness fell as the skirl of the Irish pipes broke out, playing a marching tune. The Munsters were wild with enthusiasm, they were strong with the invincible strength of faith and high hope, for they had with them the vital conviction of success, the inspiration that scorns danger—which is the lasting heritage of the Irish ; theirs still and theirs to remain when great armaments and armies and empires shall be swept away, because it is immovable as the eternal stars.

. . . . . .

On the morning of May the 9th, 1915, the Third Infantry Brigade were ordered to attack. Their right was on the Cinder Track, and their left on the Orchard Redoubt. The Munster Fusiliers were the assaulting Battalion, with the 4th Royal Welsh Fusiliers ; the Gloucesters and South Wales Borderers in reserve.

The morning of the 9th broke incredibly still and fair, touching the land with the strange suggestion of unreality, which is part of the mystery of early dawn ; and the Rue du Bois, for all its desolation, was for a moment beautiful with the spaciousness of peace. Night dews were still in the air, and the first coming of the sun was not far distant when sustained thunder pervaded the whole world. The bombardment of the enemy's trenches had begun, and the noise grew to the dimensions of intensest force, crashing and roaring with the rage of a storm at sea. The object of the bombardment was to cut gaps in the barbed wire in front of the Battalion, and for seven minutes the torrent of sound tore and rent the air. Only for thirty minutes the guns spoke, and on the amazed instant of silence Colonel Rickard gave the order for attack. Cheering wildly the men followed him over the breastworks, with a rush that swept them across the open under deadly fire to a little ditch, some half-way between the British and German lines. There they were to lie down and take cover while the Artillery again bombarded, only continuing the rush when the fire lifted.

As they crossed the first hundred and fifty yards to the given point, Colonel Rickard fell, killed by a bullet that struck the spinal column of the neck. No one who knew him could ever doubt that he would have chosen any

LIEUTENANT-COLONEL V. G. H. RICKARD
2nd Royal Munster Fusiliers, killed while gallantly leading
the Battalion at Rue du Bois, 9th May, 1915

Record of Service :—South African War, 1902—Served as Adjutant, 2nd Royal Munster Fusiliers, operations in the Transvaal, April to May, 1902. Operations in Orange River Colony, February, April and May, 1902. Queen's Medal, with three clasps. Promoted Temporary Lieutenant-Colonel, 8th March, 1915.

[*To face p.* 38.

STORY OF THE MUNSTERS 39

other end than to die leading the Regiment he so loved all his life; he gained the perfect death that takes no thought of self, and which, in all truth, is swallowed up in victory.

Captain Campbell Dick, leading with magnificent dash, carried on B Company with 5 and 6 Platoons, led to admiration by Lieutenant Price and Lieutenant Horsfall; by this time the close-range fire of the Germans poured like rain from thunder-clouds. Caring nothing at all for the enemy's bullets, Captain Dick swept on, followed by his men, his great buoyant spirit lifted to the very heights by the joy of the charge. If life may truly be measured by its intensity, the Munsters lived well and dangerously in those moments. Captain Dick, gifted, as has been said of another very brave officer, " with a certain devilry of spirit " and " a ceaseless militancy in life and death," was well known to be a man of unshaken nerve and flame-like attributes; as he reached the second line of the German trenches he stood on the enemy's breastworks, quite indifferent to the danger which lay on every side, and standing as he often stood cheering a winner in the old days in Ireland, he waved his cap and shouted to his men, "Come on, the Munsters!" A moment after, he fell into the German trenches, and the Company he commanded dashed onwards with Lieutenant Price and Lieutenant Horsfall, and were enveloped in the very heart of the grey enemy forces. Lieutenant Carrigan and Lieutenant Harcourt brought the machine guns over the parapet of the German first line, and there faced an enfilading fire that beat and battered upon the men, who, without wavering, held grimly to the trenches; a little further up the line Lieutenant Sealy King died

CAPTAIN J. CAMPBELL-DICK
2nd Royal Munster Fusiliers, killed in action 9th May, 1915

Record of Service:—South African War, 1899-1902—Advance on Kimberley, including action at Belmont; operations in the Transvaal, West of Pretoria, July to 29th November, 1900; operations in Orange River Colony, May to 29th November, 1900, including actions at Linaley (27th June), Bethlehem (6th and 7th July), and Wittenbergen (1st to 29th July); operations in Cape Colony, South of Orange River, 1899-1900; operations in Transvaal, 30th November, 1900, to January, 1901; operations in Orange River Colony and Cape Colony, September, 1901, to 31st May, 1902; operations in Cape Colony, North of Orange River; Despatches, London Gazette, September 19th, 1901. Queen's Medal with three clasps; King's Medal with two clasps.

[*To face p.* 40.

most gallantly as he dashed to a renewed attack.

The Regiments on the left and right being unable to get near the line where the Munsters were fighting, the position became that of a forlorn hope; but the fighting stuff of which the Munster Fusiliers are made, does not break. Their dash and coolness drew words of admiration from the Artillery officers who were observing, and the men, almost entirely without officers or N.C.O.'s, rallied and fought with unabated courage.

Only 300 yards away was the safety of the British trenches, but between that point and where the Battalion fought the gulf might as well have been as wide as eternity.

The hail of shells and the rain of bullets never ceased, and as the time went on and the Battalion was unsupported, Major Gorham, then in command and wounded in the arm, sent a message back that the assault was held up by the great breaking superiority of the enemy's forces.

Once again the heavy guns boomed out, pitching shell after shell into the German lines, and under cover of this protective fire the Battalion withdrew. Incidents of great self-sacrifice were many during the retirement. Sergeant Gannon carried one officer and four wounded comrades out under fire; Private Barry, himself mortally wounded, and only a slight slip of a boy from Cork, brought in Captain Hawkes, one of the biggest officers in the Battalion. Captain Hawkes was severely wounded in three places, and could not move, and as he carried his officer to safety, Private Barry fell, dying heroically, his death a tribute to the feeling that so strongly existed between officers and men.

. . . . . .

So the Munsters came back after their day's work; they formed up again in the Rue du Bois, numbering 200 men and three officers. It seems almost superfluous to make any further comment.

. . . . . .

In a garden near a place called Windy Corner, Colonel Rickard is buried at the head of a line of graves. As Father Gleeson wrote: "The Munsters who gave their lives so heroically and cheerfully, have, even in death, at their head, their kindly and loving leader, who so much inspired them and cheered us all."

Honest and brave soldiers, the world must go on without you, and those who are left to mourn you must face what remains in life with a little of your own fine spirit. But your lives and your great deaths have enriched the story of the world, the story of Ireland and the story of the Battalion, even though, through all the voices and all the sounds of life, we listen for your voices, and will listen still in vain.

THE MUNSTERS AT HULLOCH
September 25th, 1915

Drawn by F. Matania.]

[To face p. 45.

THE MUNSTERS AT HULLOCH

September 25th, 1915.

"In a trench upon a battlefield of France himself
  is lying,
And shall never set potatoes any more.
Just himself and me together, in the spring and
  autumn weather,
Will not set or dig potatoes any more."

OONA BALL.

BELOW the château of Vaudricourt there is a wood which closes it around with a sense of security belonging to fir woods, and the zone of pines is dense and fragrant.

On the night of September 23rd, 1915, the Royal Munster Fusiliers marched from the little village of Philosophe and bivouacked in the Vaudricourt domain. The battalion was on the march again, and that dim, cloudy night they trooped in under the shelter and lighted their camp fires.

The whole effect was mysterious and unreal as things seen in dreams; the columns of luminous smoke soared upwards, illuminating the low strong branches of the trees, and around the fires the men lay huddled in their greatcoats, grouped within the circles of flickering light.

Just as the fires were dying down into blackness a little incident that memory dwells upon changed the Vaudricourt woods into an undying picture for those who saw it. One of the men stretched out his arm and placed a lighted candle on a branch just over his head, and as though this simple act appealed to the memories and imaginations of his comrades, in a moment the pine woods of Vaudricourt became transformed into a forest of Christmas trees. One after another the tiny flames appeared, and burned like a hundred little glittering shrines. God knows what memories of childhood and things that were far enough away from war it recalled to the hearts of these men.

Yet the memory of the clouded night, the whisper of the wind in the trees, and the woods of Vaudricourt, bright with the soldiers' candles, comes like a gleam across the vast darkness and lights again the faces of the war-worn battalion once more on its way to the fighting line.

. . . . . .

On September 24th the Munsters took up their position close to La Routoire Farm. Beyond these trenches the Germans occupied a long, sweeping ridge of down land; a space of quiet scenery spread out to the horizon like a calm sea. On the German side were Auchy, Hulloch, and Loos, and on the

British Cambrin, Vermelle, Philosophe, and Mazingarbe, and between them the desolate ground from which living things are fenced and barred out. The trenches divided the two main roads at right angles, and the Hulloch road played an important part in subsequent operations. Here and there over the grass, piles of slag stood out like stubborn towers, black and desolate as some minor, haunting fragment of an evil dream. They masked the mines, and were treacherous, cruel defences on a poor, wasted land.

The weather was gloriously fine, and under the heavy bombardment of the British guns the whole sky-line seemed to be in eruption. Huge masses of chalk-dust and smoke lifted hundreds of feet into the air, and rolled slowly away like a drowsy cloud trailing near the ground and reluctant to depart from this " best of all possible worlds."

MAJOR J. W. CONSIDINE
2nd Royal Munster Fusiliers, killed while leading the
Battalion at Hulloch, September 25th, 1915

Record of Service :—Left Sandhurst in April, 1902. Mohmand Expedition, 1908. King's Medal and clasp. France, April 11th, 1915. Took temporary command of the 2nd Battalion, May 10th.

[*To face p.* 49.

STORY OF THE MUNSTERS 49

In the grey light of the morning of September 25th the British guns opened a furious fire, joined by the rattle of rifle and machine guns. Without fuss or disorder the Munsters awaited the moment when they should face a pouring stream of bullets and charge into the teeth of the storm.

Led by Major Considine, the Munsters pushed up the winding trenches to the front line, exchanging a word or two as they went, and relying, as all men do in time of crisis, upon those unexplained resources that stand for all that is best in a soldier. When they reached the front line the leading company was blocked, for the trenches were full of men, with their faces coloured an ashen blue and the buttons and badges on their coats turned green. Some were dead and others unconscious, for they were the helpless victims of gas fumes.

When the Munsters charged over

the parapet the Hulloch road was alive with troops racing towards the German trenches, but to the front all was quiet, and a number of khaki figures in blue gas helmets lay very still out over the grass towards the German lines, having so encountered that " last and greatest of all fine sights " in the cold dimness of half oblivion.

The fire from the enemy's guns increased as the Munsters advanced with a yell, and the wire ahead of them was apparently unbroken.

Leading " A " Company, Major Considine fell in the advance, and as he sank down Sergeant-major Jim Leahy rushed forward to carry him into safety. He, too, was hit through the heart by a German bullet, and when he fell the advancing Munsters cheered him as they raced ahead, carrying with them the memory of the two men who had fallen so gallantly, into their fierce charge. Both Major Considine and Sergeant-major Leahy are buried on the battlefield almost where they fell, 800 yards west of Vermelles.

Up the long-deserted, grass-grown Hulloch road six batteries came at a gallop, wheeling boldly across the open under heavy fire, the Munsters, in conjunction with the brigade, following at a run. Great volcanoes of black smoke shot up immediately as the bombers worked down the German trenches. Lieutenant Denis Conran with six of his company occupied a support trench crowded with German troops, and for forty-eight hours held this small salient of the advance, waging a steady war with unwavering determination and grit. The enemy were all around this small handful, and from where they fought they could see the village of Hulloch being knocked to pieces like a card-house, and again on the right the shell-torn havoc of the advance to Loos, the chalk pit, and Hill 70. The larger stride had been taken at last, and the men in their gas helmets with their five days' growth of beard looked strange and almost Oriental as they advanced, receded, and again advanced as the deadly conflict rolled onwards.

Towards evening the weather turned bitterly cold and heavy rain began to fall. The smell of poison gas, shell fumes, and blood became almost overpowering. Among the torn bodies the flotsam of war lay unheeded in the mud. Innumerable blankets, rifles, caps, belts, and bloodstained dressings told that a memory was all that was left to many of those who had been alive and glad a few hours before, and everywhere there were dead, dying, and wounded men, and all the helpless misery of battle.

The troops charged again, and the remnants of the Munsters raised another cheer and rallied for the last rush, and then the strain ended as you may see men pulled suddenly over at a tug-of-war. Four columns of German soldiers filed out of the trenches, holding their hands above their heads.

The road from Loos to Hulloch was clear at a cost of 1,000,000 shells and 50,000 men. A right of way was established at a price that no one can ever tell, since broken lives and hearts are not entered into any known roll of honour, and this right of way was made good by the simple valour and indomitable constancy of the ordinary man.

For them there is no return, for those who waited for them no more reason to cross the days off the calendar; stillness has intervened—the stillness that marks the passing of the mortal to immortality. Tears are useless, broken hearts useless; life will not alter because of these things. The days go on, and we with them;

those who have gone have " bought eternity with a little hour, and are not dead."

And the road is now clear from Loos to Hulloch.

THE STAND AT ETREUX

BEING AN ACCOUNT WRITTEN BY AN OFFICER
OF THE R.M.F., PRISONER OF WAR

MAINTZ-AM-RHEIN, GERMANY,
July 16th, 1915.

I SEND now, by special permission, the full account of the engagement of August 27th, 1914.

The night of the 26th the Battalion bivouacked at Fesmy with B Company (Captain Simms commanding) on outpost duty at Chapeau Rouge (Sketch A).

At 4 a.m. on the 27th D Company (Captain Jervis commanding) was sent up as a reinforcement. The rôle allotted to the Battalion was rear guard to the retiring 1st Army Corps, with the remainder of the Brigade in support.

Our general direction was Guise, and we were on the right of the Expeditionary Force, the French having occupied Bergues on our right on the 26th. At 8 a.m. on the 27th, our scouts having reported the village of Bergues evacuated, Major Charrier sent Captain Woods with A Company to occupy it. About two hours later the enemy attacked us here sharply, and on receiving this information, the Commanding Officer sent a troop of the 15th Hussars (placed together with 1 section 118 Battery R.F.A., under him for the day) as a reinforcement; at the same time he sent one platoon of A Company (Captain Rawlinson commanding) to assist his withdrawal from the East end of Fesmy.

With the exception of a portion of this platoon under Captain Emerson, which succeeded in joining up and withdrawing with Captain Woods, the

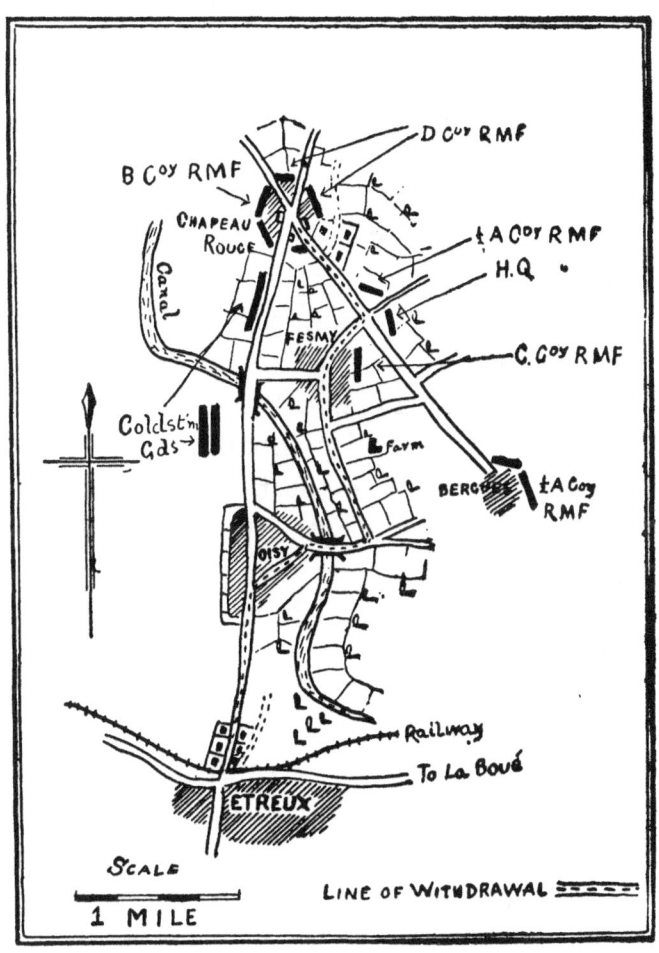

SKETCH A

remainder of the Battalion rejoined Battalion Headquarters later in the morning. The enemy was now appearing in small numbers North of Chapeau Rouge, and North-east of Fesmy. From the cross roads at Chapeau Rouge a good view of the surrounding country was obtainable, which was of a very enclosed nature, the hedges being thick and high. By 11 a.m. B and D Companies were strongly entrenched, and a brisk action began near Fesmy, and we were soon busy with rifles, machine guns, and our two 18-pounders. The enemy seemed to be advancing mainly from the North-east and rapidly approaching the village. An enemy's aeroplane passed over the position shortly before noon, our effort to bring it down meeting with no success. A few minutes later the rain came down in torrents, and under cover of it the enemy collected to attack Chapeau

Rouge. This attack commenced at 1 p.m., and having carried out our object of delaying the enemy, the two Companies engaged withdrew on Fesmy without loss, and having arrived there took up their position in support of the remainder of the Battalion, which had been hotly engaged some time. The two guns were firing rapidly. Lieutenant Chute with his machine guns was having, as he expressed it, "the time of his life." A civilian might be pardoned for questioning whether lying full length in 6 inches of muddy water under heavy fire warranted the description.

However, he undoubtedly had some excellent targets and did remarkably well, and ammunition was not spared. Some of the enemy penetrated the village, a very dashing young German officer at their head ; he fell wounded, and some prisoners were taken.

At 2.30 p.m. the withdrawal recommenced, D Company as left flank guard, and the movement across the country was very difficult and slow, gaps having to be hacked in the hedges as the Battalion fell back.

We were all quite pleased with the result of our first brush with the enemy, which cost only six or eight wounded. B Company was detailed as right flank guard and occupied a group of farm buildings some 1,500 yards from Fesmy. We thought our troubles over for the day, but Major Charrier, who took no chances, issued careful orders for the continuation of our withdrawal, B Company in advance and C Company rearguard. We passed through Oisy, fired at by a few Cavalry, C Company remained behind to hold the village of Oisy while we " made good " the rise to the South. We were hardly clear when the enemy attacked again, Captain Rawlinson holding the East and Lieutenant Awdry the Northern exits. Our two guns and two Maxims replied vigorously, and the cross-fire which resulted must have been pretty damaging. Offers of assistance were refused, and C Company withdrew successfully and proceeded to rejoin. Before they could do this a heavy fire from rifle and Maxim guns was opened on us from East and South, and it became obvious that we were cut off. Our guns galloped South for the purpose of coming into action ; as they passed a house a shell crashed into them and a second struck the team, knocking out three or four gunners and two horses; the remainder dismounted, and in the face of a murderous fire brought their guns into action. In addition to the artillery and rifle fire from the East, a raking rifle fire took us in flank from the environs of Etreux, and it was this

62 STORY OF THE MUNSTERS

position the Commanding Officer decided to attack. Lieutenant O'Malley was sent to C Company to direct them to keep the road clear as Lieutenant Chute was to open fire with his machine guns at the enemy advancing from North. Lieutenant O'Malley bicycled back under heavy fire, and a couple of ammunition carts came up to us at a gallop before the horses were shot, indeed a gallant feat.

B Company, with half A Company in support, shook out to attack. The enemy was located in a loopholed house on the West side of the road (see Sketch B), and also in the near fields. On the other side of the road a farmhouse had caught fire and blazed furiously. The Commanding Officer, Captain Wise, and Lieutenant Mosely succeeded in approaching to within fifty yards of this house, creeping along a ditch followed by their men. The enemy's fire

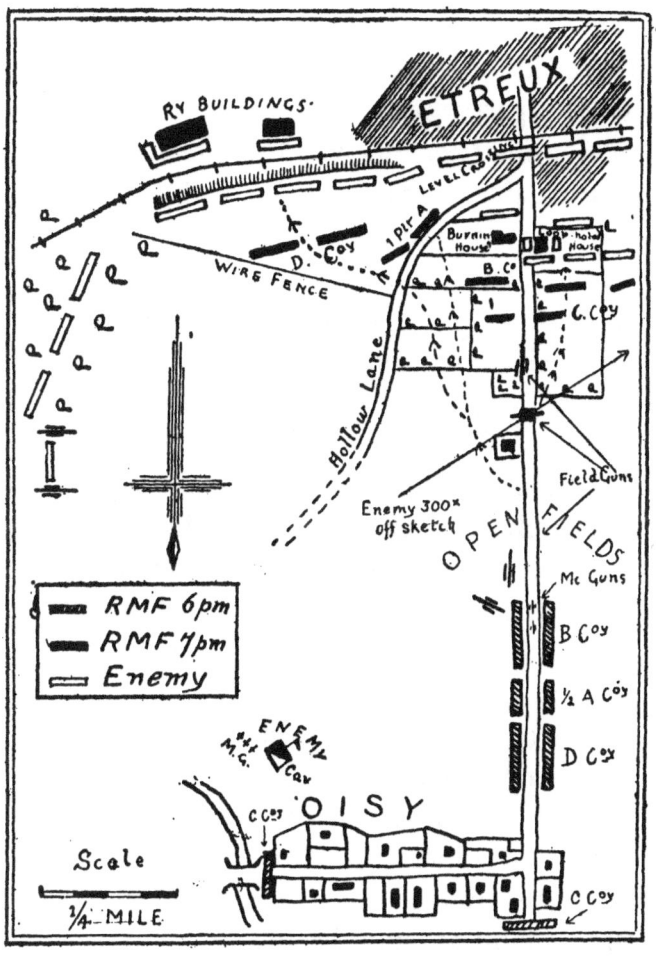

SKETCH B

was intense, and though Captain Wise succeeded in reaching the house, the whole party was put out of action. Major Charrier renewed the attack, and again later made a third attack, with his usual determination, but was shot dead at close range in the last charge. B Company was heavily engaged from both sides of the road, and Captain Simms was killed gallantly leading the attack. C Company reinforced this position, and D Company, which was in the orchard East, converged into the open and was met by a flank attack from the enemy holding the cutting. Aided by the fire of a platoon of A Company, D Company advanced by alternate rushes to within 70 yards of the hedge, where the officer in command (Captain Jervis) ordered a charge. The men sprang up with a cheer, fixed bayonets and charged. The enemy's fire redoubled, and Lieutenant Phayre fell, shot through the heart. Man after man went down, and only Captain Jervis reached the hedge alive, subsequently falling into the enemy's hands. The remnants of the Battalion fell back to the orchard where Captain Hall was wounded. Lieutenant Gower organised a defence facing N.S.E. and West. The ammunition was exhausted and most of the gunners killed, Major Bayley wounded. The enemy had entirely surrounded the Battalion, but, encouraged by the few remaining officers, the men fought on until 9 p.m. Sounds of approaching help were listened for in vain, and the Battalion, reduced to 4 officers and 256 N.C.O.'s and men, surrendered. The Battalion was engaged against 7 Battalions German Infantry, 3 Batteries, Cavalry and many Maxim guns.

Officers of the 2nd Battalion Royal Munster Fusiliers, May 1915
For names see Appendix, page 111

[*To face p.* 66.

APPENDIX

Letter from Captain H. S. Jervis, 29th August, 1914, to Mrs. Charrier

France, August 29th, 1914.

My dear Mrs. Charrier,

It is inexpressibly painful to me to have to write to you to tell you that the Major, our splendid Commanding Officer, fell in action the day before yesterday, while leading his regiment most gallantly against overwhelming odds.

The regiment was left behind, and for several hours fell back fighting under the personal direction of your husband, who, although well aware of the impossible nature of his task, issued his orders and made all arrangements with the precision which made him so well known in Aldershot.

Eventually the Germans worked round to the rear and cut us off completely, the key of their position being a loopholed house. The Major personally led two charges in a magnificent attempt to capture this. In the first of these he was wounded, but insisted upon still retaining command and cheering us on. Shortly afterwards he was wounded again, but even this did not keep him from what he considered his duty. He heroically continued the direction of the action till after sunset—six hours intermittent fighting.

Mr. Gower came up to make a report to him and found him near one of our guns which had been put out of action. In reply to Mr. Gower he said, "All right, we will line the hedge; follow me." Still leading and setting an example to all, he was shot a third time, and mortally. He fell in the road.

Yesterday we sent out a party of our men to collect and bury the dead, and they found Paul Charrier lying as he had fallen, head towards the enemy. The Sergeant told me he looked as if he was asleep. They buried him, with eight other officers of the regiment who were killed, in a grave separate from the men.

I personally received orders and made reports to him during the entire day, and never for an instant did he lead me to suspect that he was in any way worried as to our eventual safety.

The action, involving as it did the loss of an entire battalion, killed, wounded, and prisoners, may be looked on by some as a disaster, and the highest praise that I can think attainable by a commanding officer was his, in that in spite of this he retained the entire trust and confidence of all ranks to the last.

The nearest village to the action is Etreux, I think.

All his personal trinkets were buried with him. His heavier kit was on the ──── regimental transport. I believe this got away.

Six of us, officers, are prisoners here, and 500 men of the battalion, many of whom are wounded. My brother officers and the N.C.O.'s and men of the battalion ask me to tender to you and your family our deepest sympathy in your irreparable loss, which will be felt throughout the Division, but most of all in the old regiment.

  Believe me, etc.,
    Yours very sincerely,
      H. S. JERVIS.

APPENDIX

LETTER FROM CAPTAIN JERVIS, 2ND BATTALION ROYAL MUNSTER FUSILIERS, TO THE FATHER OF LIEUTENANT CAROL AWDRY, WHO WAS KILLED AT ETREUX, 27TH AUGUST, 1914

As the senior of the surviving officers of the action fought by the regiment on August 27th, it is my sad duty to have to write and inform you that your boy lost his life that day while leading his men against overwhelming odds. The Army was, at the time, withdrawing, and the battalion was occupying an important position covering the movement.

In order the better to safeguard the retreat of the remainder, our withdrawal was delayed by some hours. We were attacked on three sides, and when we moved off finally it was found that the greatly superior forces of the Germans had enabled them to cut us off from our main body. Faced by odds of six or eight to one, we put up the best fight we could until compelled by fire from all sides to surrender. E Company —to which your son belonged, of course—was chosen to watch our right rear (on the N.E.) as the battalion withdrew to the South, and Captain Rawlinson selected your son to take his platoon out to an exposed position, the far end of a village named Fesmy, through which our line of retreat lay.

He performed the duty in a most able manner, and although harassed with a nasty fire, he held on until the battalion withdrew, and then rejoined with his little force intact. It was a commendable performance, worthy of one of far greater age and experience than your son. His Company then continued the withdrawal until we came to the next village (Oisy), when it was detailed to act as rearguard. Again they were sharply engaged, by largely increased forces this time, but they gallantly held their own, your son again holding a detached position at important cross-roads, and again the battalion was able to withdraw in safety. Your boy's party was the last to come in, and though he lost a few men he saved many more. It was now six o'clock (p.m.), and it was then discovered that they were cut off from the main body. The battalion shook out to the attack in an endeavour to break through, every officer doing good work, your son no less than the others. With sword drawn, he led his men in support of the attack, which was in progress in front (to the South), and as he advanced he fell, shot through the lungs. His death was painless and practically instantaneous. He was buried with his eight brother officers, who fell the same day, in one grave.

74 STORY OF THE MUNSTERS

LETTER FROM CAPTAIN JERVIS, 2ND BATTALION ROYAL MUNSTER FUSILIERS, TO MRS. C. T. F. CHUTE

The regiment was left in a somewhat exposed position, and the orders for a withdrawal seem to have gone astray. Chuty, with his guns, which he handled during the day with really wonderful skill, covered the withdrawal of my company at mid-day. It was pouring with rain, and with entire disregard to personal comfort, characteristic of him, he lay down in six inches of water to manipulate his guns the better. The Germans were crossing the front, and he never neglected an opportunity of delaying their advance. He withdrew them from one position to another, all day forming an invaluable escort to the two field guns we had attached to us.

The withdrawal continued through a village, at about 5.30 p.m., and at the other side of it he came into action again, firing right down the road, on both edges of which Captain Rawlinson's company was withdrawing. Owing to the help of your husband's guns the company got safely through and rejoined the battalion. The enemy was now on three sides of us, and their artillery opened fire. Chuty brought his machine guns back at the gallop along the road under a positive hail of lead. It was a splendid feat and was successfully accomplished, and once again the guns were placed in position. We were now completely surrounded, and your husband tried to cross the road to try and find a target to aim at. As he crossed he was shot in the right side and thigh and fell dead.

Up to the last he was cheery and full of spirits as ever ; in fact, he was the life and soul of the mess. It is impossible to realise that we'll never hear his voice again. He will leave a large gap, not only in the regiment, but in each and all of his brother officers' hearts. It may be some small consolation to you to know that before the action he was looked upon as the best machine-gun officer of the Brigade, and his work during the day only served to confirm this view. Yesterday, the 28th, the Germans allowed us to send out a burial party of our own men, and they found Chuty, and buried him, with the eight other officers of the regiment who were killed, in a grave separate from the men. He was buried with all his personal effects on him. His heavier kit is with the regimental transport, the only part of the regiment to escape.

May I, on behalf of the surviving officers and men of the regiment, now prisoners in German hands, tender our most sincere sympathy for a loss which we know only too well is one which can never be replaced.

APPENDIX

Extract from a letter from Lieutenant Thomas written to his mother

I landed at Havre on 12th August, and we stayed in camp two days. After that we came a long way by train to Le Nouvion, and marched to a little place called Boué, where we went into billets. I stayed in a lovely old farm house, and the people were awfully good to me and fed me on the best of everything. Well, then we were marched right up to Belgium in two days—about fifty miles, to a place called Grand Rong, and the second day thirty-two miles ; the next day we fought a small battle just on the frontier, without any losses, and returned right away back to Fesing, just near where we started all the machinery ; then the real fighting started. The first I knew of it was being roused at 3 a.m. by an orderly from Headquarters, to proceed with my platoon to reinforce another Company on outpost who were being attacked; there we fought for two days, and just as we thought all was over we found we were surrounded, and a desperate battle began. I could not describe the horrors of it on paper, but we were three-fourths of a Battalion fighting six German Battalions, without any chance of relief, and I think we really did our best. We had a section of artillery and two machine-guns with us, which helped a lot, but they were very soon knocked out. Our Colonel[1] was a wonder to see. He had absolutely no fear, and I followed him and helped him all I could in every charge, but he was blown to pieces in the end by a shell. We had, I think, ten officers killed and five wounded, and the remainder prisoners. I was wounded in

[1] This refers to Major P. A. Charrier, who was in command of the Battalion.

two places—a bullet right through my throat and all the biceps of my left arm blown away by a piece of shell. My throat, of course, is bad and very troublesome. They put in a tube so as to allow me to breathe, and I can eat and drink, but I can't speak. All the officers were sent off to Germany yesterday, and the men who were able to travel, so I am alone among the Germans, except for three men, who are very bad. This town is about the size of Bandon, and is just one big hospital; every house is full of wounded, and flies, and the smells are awful. Well, although we were beaten, I believe we gave as good as we got. We killed and wounded a great many Germans, and they say themselves that we made a gallant fight of it. When I come home I will be able to tell you some strange tales, but I can't write it all. Our fellows who were in the South African War say it was child's play to this, and there never was a battle as fierce as the one we were knocked out in.

SIR A. CONAN DOYLE AND THE BATTLE OF MONS

In March 1915 Sir A. Conan Doyle gave an address on "The Great Battles of the War," in the Usher Hall, Edinburgh, to a vast and enthusiastic assemblage. The following extract from the *Scotsman* of the next morning refers to the Munsters :—

Sir Arthur, commencing with the Battle of Mons, pointed out that there the real impact of the German army fell upon two Brigades of the British. It was true that the British had fallen back from the defence of a peninsular sweep of the canal, which created "a dangerous salient" regarded from the outset as tactically indefensible ; but, when the British Commander-in-Chief received from the French the fateful telegram which compelled his retirement, the battle was in a state in which it was difficult to say who had won and who had lost. The outstanding incidents in the masterly-conducted retreat were finely told—the forced marches of the fatigued troops, "who had the depression of defeat without understanding why they had to retire " ; the heroic rearguard actions fought, notably by the Cheshires, the Gordons, and the Munsters ; the saving of the guns by the 9th Lancers ; the hopeless odds which General Smith-Dorrien encountered of three to one in men and six to one in artillery, and the dauntless defence by the remnant of L Battery. It was one of the misfortunes of a widespread action, he said, that it was very difficult to keep in touch with all units ;

they never knew what might become of their messengers. Three times in the course of the Mons retreat, first in the case of the Cheshires, then the Gordons, and thirdly the Munsters, regiments were left without orders. Messengers were shot down, and orders to retire never reached these gallant units, which fought on and on, long after their comrades had retired, until, utterly exhausted in strength and material, the remnants had to surrender. If ever in the world surrender was justifiable, he remarked, it was under these circumstances. In the case of the Cheshires, the Gordons, and the Munsters, the same thing happened, showing that great attention should be paid to the point as to how far troops lying at a distance should be notified as to what was going on.

APPENDIX

LETTER FROM LIEUTENANT-COLONEL G. J. RYAN
D.S.O., TO A FRIEND

Yes, disaster again, eight of our best officers, including those you knew—Thomson, Durand, Day, O'Brien and Pemberton—killed while gallantly leading their men ; three others, including the Colonel, wounded, and two hundred men killed and wounded. A sad story when we think of those, but a story, too, of bravery and endurance.

I will first tell you briefly what occurred, and then go on to give details which you will want to hear. The First Division marched at one hour's notice, at 6.30 p.m., on the night of Sunday, December 20th, lay down for three hours before dawn, marched out at dawn on 21st, a halt at 9 a.m. in heavy rain and cold for breakfast, and on again.

The leading Brigade deployed at

84 STORY OF THE MUNSTERS

2 o'clock for an attack in relief of the Indian Division. The Third Brigade followed, and were put in first after 2 p.m., the Welsh Regiment and the Gloucesters, supported by the Munsters and the South Wales Borderers. By dusk the Munsters were taken from support, and put out to the right to fill a gap between the Gloucesters and the next Brigade of the Division.

No food or rest came to the men with nightfall, and all that night was spent in endeavouring to recover trenches originally held by Indians from which they had been forced to retire. Before dawn came the order that all trenches not retaken, originally in British possession, must be captured, the general attack to continue at 7 a.m.

Still no food or rest for men continually under arms since Sunday night. By gallant advances, often in the open, under heavy fire, in swampy, boggy

APPENDIX

country and drenching rain, the advance continued.

The line was straightened out, but the enemy contested every foot, and only retired when he saw the attack was serious, to his original trenches. From that a continuous heavy fire was brought to bear on exhausted and heavily tried troops, but when night came on Tuesday, 23rd, the Division was firmly established in its lines, and not one foot of trench has been given up since, nor was a single British prisoner taken. The Third Brigade had a nasty bit, and the Munsters worst of all, an open bit, with dykes full of water, old trenches and bog. The attack began at 7, and by 9 they came under a wicked fire. The men went gamely on, most splendidly led by their officers, but it was no good. Officer after officer was killed, and the companies, pinned to the ground by fire, split up and extended. There they lay all day. Night came, no orders—not a man back, except some wounded who trickled back. By midnight came the order to get word out to the Munsters to get their companies to a place of safety and retire. I only got the Colonel in at 4 a.m., after two search parties had failed to find him. He had been lying there badly wounded since 10 a.m. the previous day, and so the companies got back one by one. I will now tell you how it came about I was not touched myself.

I had been out the whole of the night before with Major Thomson.

He and I insisted we would not go on into nothingness to be cut up piecemeal. We went out in the dusk towards the enemy's trenches, made a good line about a thousand yards out, sent back for spades, dug in, made good, left one company out, and were back about 4 a.m. and reported to the Colonel, who was in Reserve with the other two companies; lay down to rest for an hour or so, and the Colonel woke us saying: "Orders just come; the attack must be continued at 7 a.m., and all trenches formerly occupied by the Indians must be retaken."

Soon after 6.30 I was just going out with all the rest, and the men ready to move off, when the Colonel said to me: "Ryan, I am taking every man out on this show, and nobody quite knows where we are going or what is in front of us. I have no time to write. You must go back to Brigade Headquarters, see the General, and arrange about ammunition and transport. Collect anything you can and report where and how the Battalion is gone; the whole Brigade attacked, much split up." I collected six men, all I could find, got back to Brigade Headquarters, all under fire, reported, and was sent to fetch up doctor, stretcher bearers, ammunition, food, and stragglers, everything having disappeared in the furious advance of the previous day and night. The men were without food or water for 46 hours, except what they had on them. By 11 o'clock I was back at Brigade Headquarters, reported I had done all I could, that the Regiment had disappeared into nothingness—not a trace of them—no reports in—heavy firing everywhere. We were the right regiment of the Brigade, the first Brigade on our right, and pushed into a gap. I kept my six men and went out to locate the Battalion by yelling out, using my glasses and meeting wounded men. I sized up trouble. I went to the Brigadier and reported. He had no help to give, no men left to put in.

APPENDIX 89

I sent out again, splitting my men into patrols of two each, promised them anything if they could get to the companies and get reports.

They went out and were back again by 8 o'clock (it was dark at 4) all of them under fire, with reports. "Very few officers left, companies lying out under fire, search-lights of the enemy going up, many casualties, no orders, Colonel wounded, two Senior Majors killed. Send us orders, please." I reported to the Brigade again, saying something *must* be done, for, if still there when daybreak came, not a man would be left. All this time they were getting no support from any regiment on their right or left, in a bad gap of bog, and dyke and mud. By 9 a.m. no orders had got to me to try and get them back.

The Brigade people, quite unable to communicate with them themselves, the rest of the attack hung up by fire, and things looked rotten.

I had collected odds and ends—food, cookers, everything I could—but at my wit's end to know what to do as I realized only too well the impossible position the Regiment was in. Wounded came trickling in ; to make matters worse, it was pitch black night and beastly cold, with heavy rain—not a light or a sign or a road or a path, only dykes, knee-deep in mud and slime, and always the German rifle fire and ours, intermittent, and flames shot up like rockets by them.

It was 10 o'clock before the Brigadier's orders got to me to get orders out to them to retire, and even by then I had not a single unwounded man left of all the four companies that had gone out at 7 a.m. to show me where they had got to. Once more I called on my trusty six who had located them at dusk,

APPENDIX 91

and sent them out in three parties, again with definite orders to come back to me at a certain point where I was alone but for a few stray men and no officers.

By midnight, to my relief, I got the remnant of the four companies in, worn out, scattered, and starved, as their officers had fallen and many men in the advance. All they could do was to follow my guides in. I fed them and put them away. Result — wounded and some others left out. I called for volunteers and took a party out with stretchers and got some in, but we drew a blank for the Colonel and Major Thomson. The Adjutant had come in not wounded, but dead beat, and could not quite say where the Colonel was. At 2 a.m., or nearly 3, I think it was, I went round again and collected the exhausted non-commissioned officers who had come in, called for volunteers again, put the machine-gun officer in charge, and said, "Do not come back without the Colonel and Major Thomson." I had some bad suspense until the party returned carrying the Colonel wounded and poor Thomson dead. All the rescue work was done under rifle fire and many wounded brought in. All next day we could not get more, the ground so swept by fire. At dusk I moved them to a village 1½ miles in rear of Brigade Reserve. From that day on we have two companies out of four at a time always in trenches about one mile from our disaster; eternal sniping and shooting, no one can move up to the trenches by day. Rain had fallen still, in torrents, the trenches knee-deep in water. I have had many sick since Christmas Day. Last night I had three killed in relieving. To-night I took the two relieving companies up myself, right off the road into bog and dirt, but off the beaten track, and got the relief through with no loss. The Colonel is at Boulogne and doing well there. Of the officers the last two regulars left have knocked up since Christmas and must go home.

I am keeping fit and well, having what I want, responsibility and command, and have just got to do my best to get officers and men through, now that the best of our officers are gone. Night and day are the same, the indoor part spent in the most utterly be-shelled and ruined village you can imagine, and every other mark a shell or bullet hole. I had eight of the saddest letters to write home, besides three others of news of the wounded, but have not had time to write a full account to anyone but you, and that not until tonight, when I feel fitter and not so tired, but you will tell all who want to know—all who care for the Regiment and feel for the losses—all they may be proud to hear, that the Regiment did all and more than they could; the officers killed all died most gallantly leading their men, and the men did all that men could do—played up splendidly. I have never known men do so much, and I am very proud of them. In a special order by Sir Douglas Haig he mentioned the Munsters first in order. He said:—" Seldom have troops so nobly responded to such a test of their bravery and endurance."

Letter from Q.M.-Sergeant Wainwright, 2nd R.M.F. (since promoted 2nd Lieutenant for distinguished service in the field), to Colonel D. G. Johnston, late R.M.F.

27th January, 1915.

We were making preparations for spending our Christmas at this place, and giving the men as good a show as

APPENDIX 95

possible. On the evening of the 20th December, at 6 p.m., we received the order to march at 6.15 p.m. It was a bit of a rush, but in spite of short notice we marched to time.

The night was very cold, and about 10 p.m. it started to rain, which added very much to the men's discomfort, as the roads were in a fearful state and over ankle deep in mud; about 2 a.m. on the morning of the 21st December we got a two hours halt and rested in a broken-down factory as best we could. Marching again at 4 a.m. we kept on the move until 10 a.m., and were then kept lying about the road soaked to the skin—as the rain had not ceased since the previous night—waiting orders to move on. These orders came about 3 p.m., when we found that we were to go into the trenches.

Early on the morning of the 23rd, the order came that the trenches which had once been occupied by our troops, and were at this time in the enemy's hands (having been lost by native troops) were to be taken at any cost. The attack started at 7 a.m., led by Colonel Bent, Major Thomson being second in command. The following officers were commanding companies:—

"A" Company—Captain Woods; "B" Company—Major Day; "C" Company—Captain Hugh O'Brien; "D" Company—Major Ryan, D.S.O.

The ground to be crossed was very open country, and owing to the heavy rains a very sea of mud. From this you will understand the task the Munsters were put to. Two nights and a day with only two hours rest, and in this case very little food. Add to this the wet and cold, which was intense.

The attack was carried out, well controlled, and the trenches reached, but with very heavy loss; eleven officers—

APPENDIX 97

all of whom we could ill afford to lose—and 240 rank and file.

On the night of the 23rd, about 11.30 p.m., all we could muster were Major Ryan, one carriage machine-gun officer, and 150 men. Search parties were organised and sent out. Captain Pakenham was brought in wounded in three places, Captain Emerson exhausted and frost-bitten. By dawn on the morning of the 24th all who were left, including the wounded, were brought into the village, under heavy fire, in a thoroughly exhausted condition. The communication trench was waist-deep in water and mud, and some of the poor wounded had to be actually dug out of this quagmire.

The following day we moved to a different part of the line, and were in the trenches until the 8th January, when we were relieved for a rest until the 13th, when we again came up to the trenches, where we are now hard at it, with not much likelihood of another rest for some days to come. Since the 13th, up to date 27th, we have lost, including a few men to hospital, one officer (Major Ryan, D.S.O., shot dead) and 140 men.

On the 25th the enemy made a general attack along the whole of our line. This was evidently paving the way for the surprise birthday gift to the Kaiser on the 27th. About 6 a.m. on the 25th the attack was started with a heavy rifle and machine-gun fire, and then all our positions were shelled with heavy guns. Under the fire of these the attack was pressed home, but although some Regiments had to vacate their trenches owing to force of numbers, counter attacks were made and the positions re-taken.

You will be glad to hear that in this attack made by the enemy the *Munsters did not lose an inch*, but hung to their ground in spite of the heavy cannonade, which lasted some five hours. We were congratulated by the Brigadier and Sir John French for the splendid work done, and were fortunate enough to lose very few men, and mostly slight wounds.

Major King, who is at present commanding, slightly wounded by shrapnel in the arm, and also two young officers just joined but not belonging to the Regiment, received slight cuts from shell splinters. Major Ryan was killed returning from his visit to the trenches about 11 a.m. on the 23rd. After he was hit he only lived some few minutes, but was unconscious to the end. He was an officer of exceptional abilities, and when the news of his death spread everyone in the Brigade, from the General down, owned to having lost one of the best men here. He never spared himself for a minute, and was always doing all he could for the comfort of his men—spending a lot of his time in the trenches among the men. On returning from one of these visits he was shot.

I have not given you the names of the officers who fell on the 23rd, as they have already appeared in the *Gazette*. Colonel Bent was hit in the front line of trenches, also Major Thomson, who fell across the trench when wounded; he would not allow himself to be moved, but lay there directing operations until late in the evening, when he was again hit, this time the wound being fatal. Captain O'Brien was hit first badly, but turned to his men saying, "Now is your chance to get your own back, boys." He fell forward and died facing the enemy. Major Day was also killed leading his men and died fighting to the end.

6th February, 1915.

I had to stop writing this letter on the 27th January, owing to another attack on our lines, followed by a counter attack, in which our troops succeeded in dislodging the enemy, inflicting heavy loss and taking some ground. Our Brigade was relieved a few days after. We are now in a village billeted, resting and reorganising. The regiment was again addressed by the Brigadier yesterday and thanked for their work, and before going the General said from the look of the men it would hardly be credited that only a few hours ago they were in the trenches in very severe weather and trying conditions. It is wonderful to see the great change a few days' rest works on our men, and they now look fit for anything.

Major Rickard arrived yesterday, and

has taken over command of the Battalion from Major King of the 4th Battalion.

At present we are having very fine weather, and we all hope it continues, as it will give the men in the trenches a chance to dry themselves and make their trenches more inhabitable. The rains have been so heavy, add to this the sudden bursts of thaw and frost, the country is like a large jelly, and it is almost impossible to keep the trenches from falling in, especially under heavy shell fire, and one has to be constantly throwing back the falling earthy liquid with scoops and improvised ladles made of old tin biscuit boxes, etc.; yet in spite of all this hardship the men are in wonderful spirits, and laugh and joke through it.

APPENDIX

OFFICERS IN ACTION AT FESTUBERT

Lieut.-Colonel A. M. Bent, wounded.
Major E. P. Thomson, killed.
Major F. I. Day, killed.
Major G. J. Ryan.
Captain A. Gorham.
Captain G. A. Woods.
Captain H. C. H. O'Brien, killed.
Captain W. Emerson.
Captain R. E. M. Pakenham, died of wounds.
Captain F. W. Durand, killed.
Captain F. W. Grantham.
Captain O. Pemberton, killed.
Lieutenant J. F. O'Brien, killed.
Lieutenant H. H. Lake.
Lieutenant W. E. Molesworth, wounded.
Second Lieutenant C. H. Carrigan.
Second Lieutenant R. A. Young, killed.
Second Lieutenant T. Price.
Second Lieutenant W. J. King, wounded.

Officers not in the action but present with the Battalion at the time :—

Major A. E. King (Regimental Transport Officer).
Lieutenant W. J. Hewett (Temporary Brigade Transport Officer).
Lieutenant P. Devanney (Quartermaster).

TOTAL CASUALTIES

OFFICERS

Killed . . . 8   Wounded . . . 3

N.C.O's. AND MEN

Killed . . . 21   Wounded . . . 105
Wounded and Missing 5
Missing . . . . : . . . 61

LETTER FROM SERGEANT-MAJOR RING, 2ND R.M.F., TO COLONEL A. M. BENT, C.M.G.

The Battalion had about eight miles to march to the trenches, and the Brigadier rode with Major V. G. H. Rickard at the head, and was delighted with the men and the high spirits they were in. At 5 a.m. the artillery started the bombardment, which lasted half an hour, to cut the wire in front of the Germans' first line. The infantry went forward to the attack — the Welsh Regiment and ours were the assaulting Battalions. At 5.30 the assault took place. When the C.O. gave the order for the attack, every officer and man mounted the parapet with a cheer. It was really magnificent to see the way they attacked; every man tried to beat the others to get there first, and were splendidly led by their officers. Major Rickard was so delighted at the way the men went about their work that he could not stay, as he had arranged, to go forward with the second line. He cleared the parapet, but did not go far, as he was hit by a bullet through the spinal column of the neck. Death was instantaneous. B Co., led magnificently by Captain Dick, 5 and 6 Platoons, led by Second Lieutenants Price and Horsfall, charged and succeeded in reaching the German trenches, under a hellish fire from artillery and machine-guns. Captain Dick, as he reached the parapet of the enemy's trenches, turned and waved his cap, encouraging his men, and then went forward again, and just as he was about to enter the trench he was hit, and tumbled into the trench. Another brave officer—his fate is unknown at present. Second Lieutenants Horsfall and Price, with what was left of the platoons, cleared the first line of trenches and went to attack the second line. They were not seen again. A and B Co.'s, who were assaulting, lost all their officers and N.C.O.'s before covering half the ground. The supporting companies, C, D, came under a terrible fire, and lost all their officers and a good many N.C.O.'s, so eventually

had to retire. Out of the two platoons of B Co. who succeeded in doing their job, only three men came back. The way the Battalion behaved under the terrible fire directed against them drew words of admiration from the artillery officers who were observing. We were the only regiment in the Brigade who succeeded in doing the job we were put to do, but eventually found ourselves in the same place as we started, with only three officers left — Captain Filgate (Adjutant), Lieutenant Carrigan, and Second Lieutenant Harcourt (machine-gun officers). About 12 noon we were relieved in the first line by the 1st Brigade. Major-General Haking, Commanding the —— Division, expressed his appreciation of the splendid conduct of the Battalion in the following terms :
" The G.O.C., —— Infantry Brigade.—
. . . I wish you also to convey to the C.O., 2nd Battalion Royal Munster

Fusiliers, my appreciation of the fine example set to the Division by the successful assault of part of the leading line—a feat of arms which the Battalion must always be proud of, as this Battalion was the only one in the Brigade whose men succeeded in storming the enemy's breastworks." For great gallantry and leading, I think Captain Dick, Second Lieutenants Price and Horsfall, also the N.C.O.'s and men that followed them, deserve the greatest distinction going ; also, if any one earned a V.C., Sergeant Gannon (machine-gun sergeant) and Private Barry did. Sergeant Gannon went out several times and brought wounded men in, also a wounded officer; Private Barry, although wounded twice, brought in Captain Hawkes, who was severely wounded in three places and could not move. Poor Barry lost his life, as he was hit again while bringing in Captain Hawkes, and died from

APPENDIX 109

wounds. Except in a few cases of exceptional gallantry, every man was a hero, and I hope this time will meet with the recognition they deserve. The total casualties are as follows (all ranks) :—Killed, 46 ; wounded, 205 ; missing, 128 ; total, 379.

EXTRACT FROM LETTER TO MRS. VICTOR RICKARD FROM SERGEANT LOUIS MOORE, DATED MIDNIGHT, 25TH MAY, 1915

DEAR MADAM,

I have just returned from the trenches, and Captain Filgate told me you would like me to write you.

Since this terrible war commenced we have had many losses, as you know, but I do not believe any one has been as severely missed as he has. I believe Captain Filgate told you all about the funeral, and the spot where he was buried. I visited the little graveyard yesterday and saw everything was well.

Later I intend to get a photo of it and will send it on to you. The cross is marked in paint and inscribed—

R. I. P.
VICTOR G. H. RICKARD,
Commanding 2nd Royal Munster Fusiliers,
Killed in action, 9/5/1915.

In case anything should happen to me, I have marked the exact place on my map. Did Captain Filgate tell you how nice he looked after death? If not let me tell you. Through all the war I have seen no one who looked so much at peace. As in life, he looked bonny. I know, and am certain, that he met his death in friendship with the whole world. That he was happy at the moment I also know, for when he saw the way our brave men jumped from the breastworks and started the charge, he was overjoyed.

I am enclosing two pictures. It was

quite late when I took them. However, I know you will like them ; they were the last he had taken. Perhaps you would like to know the names of the officers.

Front row (sitting) left to right :— Lieutenant Horsfall (missing, believed killed), Lieutenant Keating (wounded), Captain Hewett (killed), Lieutenant Harcourt, Lieutenant Page (killed), Lieutenant Carrigan, Lieutenant Dennys (killed). Seated — Captain Grantham (killed), Captain Dick (missing, believed wounded), Major Gorham (wounded), Captain Filgate, Captain Fitzpatrick (wounded), Captain Hawkes (wounded). Standing (left to right)—Lieutenant King (killed), Lieutenant Parker (killed), Lieutenant Conran, Lieutenant Wainwright (wounded), Lieutenant Rabone, Lieutenant Moore (wounded), Captain Daly (wounded), Lieutenant Stokes, Lieutenant Pottinger (killed), Lieutenant Price (missing), Captain Jeffries, Lieutenant Steward (believed killed).

NOTE.—Regretted that the death of the following officers has since been ascertained :—Captain Dick, Lieutenant Stewart, Lieutenant Horsfall.

EXTRACT FROM LETTER FROM SERGEANT
LOUIS MOORE, 2ND R.M.F.

On his way up to our position on that Saturday evening, and just before reaching our trenches, we passed one of those little shrines. The Major halted his Regiment, and the Father, still mounted, gave the whole Regiment a general absolution. After that they sang the *Te Deum*. I know you can see the whole picture. The semi-light, the Major on his horse in front, and the whole Regiment uncovered. It was a sight never to be forgotten. I remember once seeing such a picture of the

APPENDIX

Irish Guards praying before they went into action.

Rue du Bois, 9th May, 1915.

CONGRATULATIONS FROM THE GENERAL OFFICERS COMMMANDING 1ST CORPS AND 1ST DIVISION, TO THE 3RD INFANTRY BRIGADE

The G.O.C.,
3rd Infantry Brigade.

I am directed by the G.O.C. 1st Army and the G.O.C. 1st Corps, to express to the Officers, N.C.O.'s, and men of the 3rd Infantry Brigade their deep appreciation of the efforts of all ranks to carry by assault the enemy's defences in front of the Rue Du Bois on the 9th May.

On my own behalf I shall be glad if you will tell Commanding Officers to inform their Battalions that nothing could have exceeded the gallantry displayed by Officers and other ranks in the assault.

I deeply regret the casualties which occurred, but they were not in vain. The men who fell afford the rest of us a fine example of how such an assault should be delivered. From a military point of view the attack was of the greatest value, because it drew away hostile reinforcements urgently required to repel the successful French attacks to the South. These reinforcements coming up towards our front formed an excellent target for our heavy guns, who fired on them with great effect.

(Sd) R. HAKING, Major-General,
Comdg. 1st Division.
1st Division H.Q.
11th May, 1915.

APPENDIX 115

ORDER OF THANKS TO ALL RANKS SERVING UNDER HIM FROM THE BRIGADIER-GENERAL COMMANDING 3RD INFANTRY BRIGADE

BRIGADE ROUTINE ORDERS,
BY BRI.-GENERAL H. R. DAVIES,

Commanding 3rd Infantry Brigade,
11*th May*, 1915.

Brigadier-General Davies wishes to thank all Battalions of the Brigade for the splendid manner in which they attacked on the 9th May. Though the attack did not succeed, it has been recognised by all the higher Commanders that the Brigade did all that could have been done. The loss of so many gallant officers and men testifies to the courage of the troops. It was a day of which all can be proud, and the Brigadier is confident that the same fine spirit will be displayed in the future.

 (Sd) C. BERKELEY, Captain,
  Brigade Major, 3rd Infantry Brigade.

Special Appreciation of the Gallantry of the 2nd Battalion Royal Munster Fusiliers, from their Divisional Commander

The G.O.C.,
3rd Infantry Brigade

I wish you also to convey to the O.C. 2nd Battalion Royal Munster Fusiliers, my appreciation of the fine example set to the Division by the successful assault of part of his leading line ; a feat of arms which the Battalion must always be proud of, as this Battalion was the only one in the Brigade whose men succeeded in storming the enemy's breastworks.

(Sd) R. HAKING, Major-General,
Comdg. 1st Division.

Printed in Great Britain by Richard Clay & Sons, Limited
Brunswick St., Stamford St., S.E. 1, and Bungay, Suffolk.

www.ingramcontent.com/pod-product-compliance
Lightning Source LLC
Chambersburg PA
CBHW031149160426
43193CB00008B/300